## SERIES TITLES

Smaller illustrations: Studio Stalio (Alessandro Cantucci, Fabiano Fabbrucci, Margherita Salvadori)

Maps: Paola Baldanzi

Photos: Bridgeman Art Library, London/Farabola Foto, Milan p. 9; Frank Teichmann, Stuttgart p. 10tr; Corbis/Contrasto, Milan p. 38b; Foto Scala, Florence pp. 42–43b

Art Director: Marco Nardi

Layouts: Rebecca Milner

Project Editor: Loredana Agosta

Research: Claire Moore

Repro: Litocolor, Florence

Consultants: Dr. Aidan M. Dodson is a Research Fellow in the Department of Archaeology and Anthropology at the University of Bristol where he teaches Egyptology. He has published over a hundred articles in various journals and magazines, written or co-written eight books, and given many lectures all over the world.

Dr. Monica Berti is a Research Fellow at the Department of History at the University of Turin. Trained in ancient history, epigraphy and papyrology, she has written numerous articles for scientific journals and has attended conferences and seminars in Italy and abroad.

ANCIENT EGYPT AND GREECE
was created and produced by McRae Books Srl
Via del Salviatino, 1 — 50016 — Fiesole (Florence), (Italy)
info@mcraebooks.com
www.mcraebooks.com

Publishers: Anne McRae, Marco Nardi
Series Editor: Anne McRae
Author: Neil Grant
Main Illustrations: MM comunicazione (Manuela Cappon, Monica Favilli) pp. 10–11, 25, 30–31, 33, 34–35, 37; Giacinto Gaudenzi pp. 22–23; Paolo Ghirardi pp. 14–15; Alessandro Menchi pp. 26–27; Leonardo Meschini pp. 20–21; Antonella Pastorelli pp. 6–7; Paola Ravaglia pp. 19, 28–29, 41; Claudia Saraceni pp. 44–45; Sergio pp. 12–13

Library of Congress Cataloging-in-Publication Data

Grant, Neil, 1938-
    Ancient Egypt and Greece / Neil Grant.
        p. cm. -- (History of the world)
    Includes index.
    Summary: "A detailed overview of the history of the Ancient Greek and Ancient Egyptian civilizations, through the age of Alexander the Great"--Provided by publisher.
    ISBN 978-8860981585
    1. Egypt--Civilization--To 332 B.C.--Juvenile literature.
2. Greece--Civilization--To 146 B.C.--Juvenile literature. I. Title.
    DT61.G679 2009
    932--dc22

                                    2008008401

Printed and bound in Malaysia

# HISTORY

# Ancient Egypt and Greece

## Neil Grant

Consultants:  Dr. Aidan M. Dodson, FSA, Research Fellow, Department of Archeology and Anthropology, University of Bristol and Dr. Monica Berti, Research Fellow, Department of History, University of Turin

Zak
BOOKS

# Contents

*Minoan bronze sculpture of a bull-jumper. As the subject appears so often in art, bull-jumping must have been important.*

*Note—This book shows dates as related to the conventional beginning of our era, or the year 1, understood as the year of the birth of Jesus Christ. All events dating before this year are listed as BCE (Before Current Era). Events dating after the year 1 are defined as CE (Current Era).*

## TIMELINE

| | 4000 BCE | 3000 BCE | 2000 BCE | 1000 BCE |
|---|---|---|---|---|
| **ANCIENT EGYPTIANS**  | | The city of Hierakonpolis develops in Lower Egypt. / Menes, the first pharaoh, unites Upper and Lower Egypt. The first Dynasty is founded. | The Great Pyramid at Giza is built. / Pharaoh Ahmose I reunites the divided kingdoms of Egypt. | Pharaoh Ramesses III defends Egypt from foreign invaders. / Egypt is divided. |
| **AFRICAN KINGDOMS**  | | Egyptians send military expeditions into Nubia to mine gold. | The Kingdom of Kush is founded in Nubia. / Kush becomes an Egyptian province. | Queen Hatshepsut sends an expedition to Punt. |
| **THE MINOANS**  | | The Bronze Age begins in the Aegean. | Rise of Minoan civilization on island of Crete. / The Minoans rebuild Crete after widespread destruction. | Mycenaeans take over Crete. |
| **THE MYCENAEANS** | | Mycenaean ancestors settle in Greece. | Rise of Mycenaean civilization. | Mycenaeans capture Troy. / End of Mycenaean civilization. |
| **ANCIENT GREEKS**  | | | | Period of migrations in the Aegean. / The city-state of Sparta is founded. |
| **THE MACEDONIANS**  | | | | |

# Introduction

Ancient Egypt, founded about 5,000 years ago, was the world's first nation-state. It was also the longest-lived, lasting about 2,500 years, far longer than any European state. Ancient Greece reached a peak as Egypt was declining. It marks the beginning of European civilization. Democratic government began in the Greek city-states, and Greek culture was to be a powerful influence on Europe until modern times. The Ancient Greeks admired the skills and understanding of the Egyptians (the Egyptian calendar, for example, was more scientific than the Greek). As early as the 7th century BCE, Greek merchants set up a settlement in Egypt, the source of much trade. Egypt influenced the Greeks in other ways, possibly in religion, certainly in art. Greek sculpture of the Archaic Period is clearly based on Egyptian style, although the Greeks soon developed new ideas. After the invasion of Alexander the Great in 332 BCE, Egypt itself became part of the Hellenistic (Greek) world. Alexandria succeeded Athens as the center of Hellenistic learning, and the last pharaohs, of the Ptolemiac Dynasty, were Greek-speaking descendants of one of Alexander's generals.

*A gold figure of an Egyptian pharaoh with the symbols of kingship —a crown, with the protective cobra and vulture, and a crook and flail.*

| 800 BCE | 600 BCE | 400 BCE | 200 BCE | 1260 | 1 CE |
|---|---|---|---|---|---|
| Nubian kings undertake building work at Thebes, Memphis, and other religious centers. | Egypt is taken over by the Persians. | | Alexander the Great conquers Egypt. | | Egypt becomes a Roman province. |
| | | | Ptolemy I, general of Alexander the Great, rules Egypt. | | |
| Nubians rule Egypt as the 25th Dynasty. | | | | | |
| | The Kushite capital is established at Meroe. | | | | |
| | | | | Greece is taken over by the Romans. | |
| The first Olympic Games are held. | | Athens and Sparta battle in the Peloponnesian War. | | | |
| The Archaic period. | Beginning of democracy in Athens. | Philip II, King of Macedonia conquers Greece. | | | |
| The Macedonian kingdom is founded. | | Alexander the Great invades Persia. | | | |
| | | | Macedonians are defeated by the Romans. | | |
| | | | Macedonia becomes a Roman province. | | |

# Early Egyptian Civilization

In the third century BCE, an Egyptian priest named Manetho (active c. 300 BCE) made a record of the 31 Egyptian dynasties covering 2,800 years. We still follow his system, but we also divide Egyptian history into periods, as shown in the box (left). Ancient writers often described Egypt and its great buildings, but most of what we know today was discovered in the last 200 years, especially since Egyptian writing, called hieroglyphs, was first deciphered in 1822. Thanks to the work of archeologists, and the evidence of tombs and temples, we know more about the Egyptians than any other ancient society.

*The Narmer Palette. Slate palettes were made for grinding minerals to powder, perhaps for cosmetics.*

### Predynastic Egypt
The first signs of Egyptian civilization appeared, long before the pharaohs, in Upper Egypt. By 3500 BCE, Hierakonpolis, the capital, was a large, lively city of mud or stone houses. It contained the first temple, the model for the great temples of the pharaohs. At the same time, a different society developed in Lower Egypt, in the Nile Delta. Its center was the town of Buto, first discovered by archeologists only 20 years ago.

*A female figure from the Predynastic, or prehistoric, age.*

*Foreigners thought the Egyptians were lucky: the Nile gave them plenty of food without too much hard work.*

### United Egypt
The first pharaoh was Menes (or Narmer), King of Upper Egypt. He conquered Lower Egypt and united the Two Lands in about 3150 BCE. Legend says he ruled for 60 years, until he was killed by a hippopotamus. He may be the king shown on the carved slate known as the Narmer Palette. On the side shown above he is wearing the "White Crown" of Upper Egypt (his prisoner may represent the north of Egypt). On the other side, which has more scenes of conquest, he wears the "Red Crown" of Lower Egypt.

## ANCIENT EGYPT

Fertile area

MEDITERRANEAN SEA

BUTO
NILE DELTA
LOWER EGYPT
GIZA    MEMPHIS
SAQQARA

RIVER NILE

THEBES
HIERAKONPOLIS

UPPER EGYPT

### The River Nile

*Egypt would not have existed without the Nile River. The longest river in the world, it ran for over 3,728 miles (6,000 km) through dry, barren desert, creating a strip of fertile land along its banks. About 93 miles (150 km) from the coast, it spread out into a delta, watering the broad plain of Lower Egypt. The Nile was a mystery. Unlike other rivers, it flooded in the summer and no one knew where the water came from. Explorers discovered the sources of the Nile in East Africa just 150 years ago. We now know that the summer monsoon caused the flood.*

*Cattle being carried across the River Nile by boat. The ancient Egyptians may have been the first people to keep cattle.*

### The Waters of the Nile

The Egyptians divided the year into three seasons, based on the behavior of the river. Summer was the time of the flood, when the Nile overflowed and deposited rich black silt. In fall, the flood went down and farmers planted their seeds. Spring was the "Dry Time," when they harvested the crops. But nature is unreliable. If the flood was too low, there was not enough fertile soil. If it was too high, it flooded the villages.

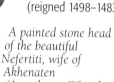

*The throne of the pharaoh Tutankhamun, found in his tomb. Made of gold-plated wood, it has a scene of the young king and his wife on the back.*

### Royal Women

The title of the pharaoh's senior partner, who was sometimes of royal birth, but was usually the daughter of a non-royal official, was the "Great Royal Wife." Her main task was to produce an heir to continue the dynasty. But some, like Nefertiti (whose husband reigned 1350–1334 BCE), were powerful figures, who shared the royal power (see page 23). There were even three female pharaohs, of whom the greatest was Hatshepsut (reigned 1498–1483 BCE).

### The Divine Pharaoh

The pharaoh was not only the ruler, he was also a god. He was seen as a form of the falcon-headed Horus, the royal god, and sometimes as the sun god, Ra. He had no private life; everything he did was a ceremony, every incident had some meaning. Even washing his hands was a religious act and, if he caught a cold, it was a bad omen for the kingdom.

*The king was also head of the Egyptian army, and his power over foreign enemies is shown by the bound images of enemies on the side of his throne (above).*

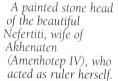

*A painted stone head of the beautiful Nefertiti, wife of Akhenaten (Amenhotep IV), who acted as ruler herself.*

# The Rulers of Egypt

The supreme ruler of Egypt was the king, also called "pharaoh" and other titles. He was also the chief priest. As the all-powerful ruler of the country with a horde of officials and servants, he was able to carry out huge projects, such as building a pyramid, or digging a canal to the Red Sea. Pharaoh could do no wrong, but he was no selfish dictator. He was protector of the people, the representative of good order, and the enemy of chaos.

*Statue of a vizier. He looks well fed.*

### Government

The pharaoh owned the country; in a sense he was the country. In practice he was served by hundreds of officials, headed by the vizier. Some viziers, even if non-royal, were very grand, as their fine tombs suggest. Imhotep, chancellor of Djoser (reigned 2630–2611 BCE) and architect of the step pyramid at Saqqara, later became a god. Women sometimes served in official posts: we know of two female viziers.

## FAMOUS PHARAOHS

**Khufu**
*(reigned 2589–2566 BCE)*
*Also known as Cheops, he ordered the building of the Great Pyramid at Giza, his own tomb, in 2500 BCE.*

**Mentuhotep II**
*(reigned 2010–1998 BCE)*
*During the Middle Kingdom he restored the unity of Egypt.*

**Kamose**
*(reigned 1573–1570 BCE)*
*Began to expel the 15th Dynasty, a line of foreign rulers from Lower Egypt.*

**Queen Hatshepsut**
*(reigned 1498–1483 BCE)*
*She sought to assert her power through propaganda reliefs. She was depicted as a man with a king's regalia, complete with the official false beard.*

**Akhenaten**
*(reigned 1350–1334 BCE)*
*Known at the beginning of his reign as Amenhotep IV. He changed his name when he revolutionized Egyptian religion and art, also moving his capital to a brand-new city, Akhetaten (known today as Amarna).*

**Ramesses II**
*(reigned 1304–1237 BCE)*
*Warrior king who expanded the Egyptian empire, built vast temples and fathered 100 children.*

## Symbols of Kingship

Representations of a pharaoh can be recognized by the symbols of royalty. He often wears one of several crowns or a striped head cloth, with a cobra and vulture, his protectors, above the forehead. He carries one or more scepters, often a crook and flail (symbols of the god Osiris), and sometimes wears a neat false beard, attached by a cord.

*The mummified remains of Tutankhamun were placed inside a solid-gold coffin, the inner coffin of three. The one shown here is the second coffin.*

## The Pharaoh Tutankhamun

The tombs of the Egyptian kings were all raided by robbers with one exception. The entrance to the tomb of Tutankhamun (reigned 1334–1325 BCE), a ruler of the New Kingdom, was concealed and only discovered, after ten years searching, by an archeologist in 1922. It contained four chambers, each full of amazing objects of priceless materials and beautiful workmanship. It was the greatest and most valuable find ever made by archeologists.

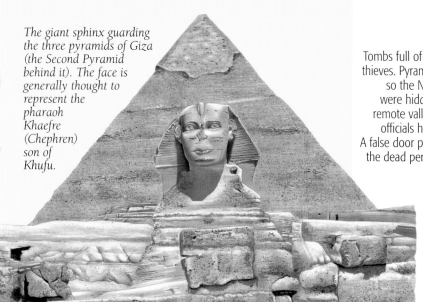

*The giant sphinx guarding the three pyramids of Giza (the Second Pyramid behind it). The face is generally thought to represent the pharaoh Khaefre (Chephren) son of Khufu.*

## Egyptian Tombs

Tombs full of valuable objects attracted thieves. Pyramids were obvious targets, so the New Kingdom royal tombs were hidden deep in the rocks of a remote valley. High-born people and officials had similar, smaller tombs. A false door painted on the wall helped the dead person's spirit go in and out.

*The walls of tombs were decorated with pictures and texts. This scene, in the Valley of the Kings, shows the pharaoh Horemheb (reigned 1321–1292 BCE) standing in front of the goddess Hathor.*

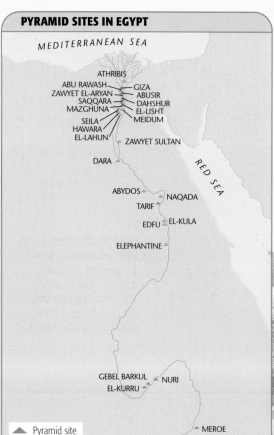

### PYRAMID SITES IN EGYPT

MEDITERRANEAN SEA

ATHRIBIS
ABU RAWASH — GIZA
ZAWYET EL-ARYAN — ABUSIR
SAQQARA — DAHSHUR
MAZGHUNA — EL-LISHT
SEILA — MEIDUM
HAWARA
EL-LAHUN — ZAWYET SULTAN

DARA

RED SEA

ABYDOS — NAQADA
TARIF
EDFU — EL-KULA
ELEPHANTINE

GEBEL BARKUL — NURI
EL-KURRU

MEROE

▲ Pyramid site

*The workers moved huge stones (one piece weighed over 1,000 tons) with ramps, poles, and ropes from the quarry to the river. Stones were then transported to the building site by boat.*

### The Pyramids

*The biggest (and oldest) buildings were the pyramids, built as tombs for the early pharaohs. The first stone pyramid (Third Dynasty), at Saqqara, had sides that rose like steps in six stages. The smooth-sided pyramids of Giza (about 2500 BCE) belong to the 4th Dynasty. The largest, the Great Pyramid of Khufu (or Cheops), is 482 feet (147 m) high, with sides 755 feet (230 m) long at the base. It contained about 2,300,000 blocks of stone, weighing nearly 6,000,000 tons. Now 4,500 years old, it has lost its smooth, glittering surface layer and about 39 feet (12 m) of its height.*

### Temples

Most of the huge temples that still stand date from the New Kingdom. They all followed the same basic plan—long and rectangular, with vast columns—and, like the pyramids, they were built on a massive scale. In area, the Great Temple of Amun at Karnak was (and is) the world's largest religious building. Temples were the houses of the gods, and only priests could go inside. Anyone wishing to consult the god had to wait until a festival, when the priests paraded his or her image outside.

# Building Egypt

The greatness of ancient Egypt is still to be seen in its monumental buildings. The Egyptians had only simple methods and feeble tools, yet these buildings would be astonishing in any age. The great temples and tombs are not especially beautiful, but they give a sense of terrific strength and power. They were built to impress people, and they were built to last for ever. Ordinary houses were made of mud bricks, a good material in a dry climate, but monumental buildings were of stone. Limestone and sandstone quarries were nearby, and granite was available, although hard to cut with copper chisels and wooden mallets.

*The Temple at Luxor, completed under Ramesses II, has colossal statues of him on the front and two rows of human-headed sphinxes lining the approach.*

### Construction Workers

With no machines, the Egyptians raised their great buildings by human muscle alone. Labor on public works was a kind of tax—all the peasants had to do it. Most of the work took place in the flood season, when they had no other tasks. The workers lived in specially built "towns." They received their pay in the form of food, drink, clothes, and other supplies.

*Part of a wall painting from a tomb showing workers making bricks from Nile mud hardened in the Sun.*

# Egyptian Society

Ancient Egypt was a society of order, where everyone belonged to a particular class. A person's place in society depended on their birth, and they followed the same occupation as their parents. Boys were taught their father's trade, and only a few learned to read and write. They were mostly the sons of scribes, who would become scribes in their turn. For pharaoh or carpenter, occupations were hereditary. People believed that life was balanced between the forces of order and justice, which they called Maat, and the forces of chaos, represented by Seth, the wild god of the desert. The duty of their god-king was to uphold this balance.

## Scribes and Officials

The scribes, or writers, were the managers, bookkeepers, and clerks of Egypt. They kept careful records of farm production, trade, taxes, and legal judgements. Training was hard, as students had to learn the great number of hieroglyphic signs. But they had important, well-paid jobs, with no hard physical work, and others envied them. "Be a scribe," said a teacher, "so your limbs may grow smooth and your hands soft."

*Scribes, with their scrolls of papyrus, appear often in Egyptian art. This ivory figure comes from the Middle Kingdom.*

## Priests

Along with the courtiers and chief officials, the high priests ranked highest outside the royal family. Priests belonged to a separate class. They were divided into many ranks, from high to low. The chief priest and his assistants performed the complicated daily rituals of the temple and organized religious festivals and processions, where the image of the god was shown to the people. Others looked after temple business, studied and taught.

*Statue of a priest from the New Kingdom wearing a leopard skin garment.*

## Taxes

Egypt was a rich country and much of its wealth went as taxes to the central government. As the Egyptians did not use money, taxes were paid in the form of produce, such as corn, and the rate of tax depended on whether the harvest was good or bad. Government inspectors went round at harvest time to calculate the tax due from each district, or nome. They were not popular!

*A faience tablet used as a label to identify a batch of scrolls.*

*Herdsmen driving cattle past a kiosk where the tax collectors count them to calculate how much is due in tax.*

*The idea of Maat was represented by a goddess, who often wore a headdress of ostrich feathers and was sometimes indicated in paintings by a single feather.*

## Justice

The law was based on the idea of Maat— what was right and orderly. The supreme judge was the pharaoh, but as in government, high officials, including priests, actually directed the justice system. Local governors, or nomarchs, judged disputes about property, contracts, wills, and such matters. Punishments could be harsh, with the death penalty for serious crimes. Minor crimes were punished by a fine or a beating.

### Gods and Goddesses

There were about 700 gods and goddesses, many only worshiped locally. Among the best known were Osiris, god of the Underworld, his wife Isis, and brother, the sinister Seth, who was defeated by falcon-headed Horus, ruler of Earth. Others widely respected were Ptah, god of craftsmen; Hathor, cow-goddess of music and pleasure; Thoth, ibis-headed god of wisdom; and Anubis, jackal-headed god of death.

*Gold figure of Amun, state god of the New Kingdom and a version of the sun god. His chief temple was at Karnak, where his festival lasted a month.*

### The Creation

The world began when Atum-Ra (the sun god), who personified life, goodness, light, and energy, arose on the "mound of creation." He created the Earth (Geb) and the Sky (Nut), and the rest of creation followed. For the Egyptians, creation was a daily happening, repeated with every rising and setting of the Sun.

*Instructed by Atum-Ra, who created him, Shu, god of the air, holds up the Sky (Nut), separating her from her husband the Earth (Geb).*

# Religion in Ancient Egypt

The purpose of religion is to explain life, and in an unscientific age religion had a lot to explain. In Egypt, religion was a part of everyday life. Temples stood at the center of society. Besides being homes for gods, they had schools, libraries, warehouses, and workshops. Priests made offerings to the gods so that they would maintain peace and security. The gods were thought to be responsible for everything that happened. Yet they were often treated as if human. A god who was thought to have failed in his duty might be "punished" by receiving no offerings for a month.

*A royal funeral procession led by the chief priest (in leopard skin). The body is carried on a papyrus boat. Funerals often had to cross the Nile River, and model boats were often placed in tombs.*

### Death and Burial

The Egyptians believed that when people died they went to a heavenly Egypt in the West. First, many ceremonies were required, supervised by Anubis (in fact by his priests). The dead person's heart was weighed against a feather, representing Maat (goddess of law, truth, and justice), to see if he were worthy. His new home was his tomb which was looked after by priests who said prayers daily, brought food, and guarded the possessions buried with him in case needed in the other world.

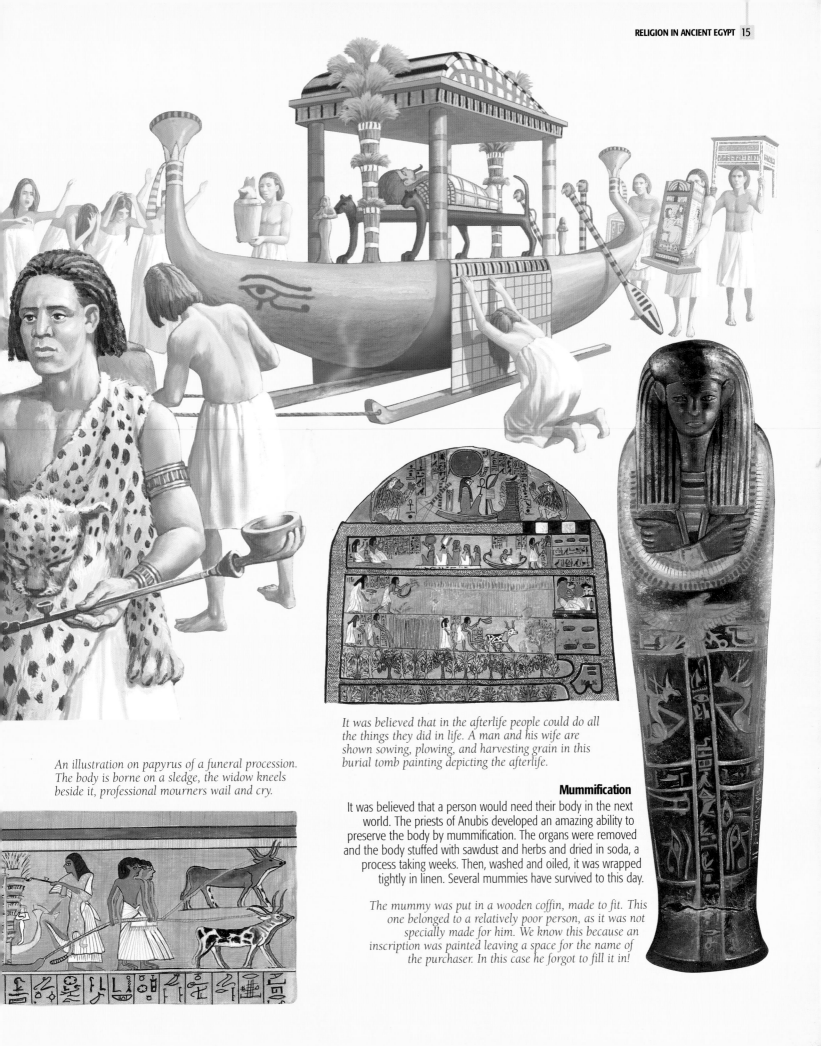

It was believed that in the afterlife people could do all the things they did in life. A man and his wife are shown sowing, plowing, and harvesting grain in this burial tomb painting depicting the afterlife.

An illustration on papyrus of a funeral procession. The body is borne on a sledge, the widow kneels beside it, professional mourners wail and cry.

## Mummification

It was believed that a person would need their body in the next world. The priests of Anubis developed an amazing ability to preserve the body by mummification. The organs were removed and the body stuffed with sawdust and herbs and dried in soda, a process taking weeks. Then, washed and oiled, it was wrapped tightly in linen. Several mummies have survived to this day.

The mummy was put in a wooden coffin, made to fit. This one belonged to a relatively poor person, as it was not specially made for him. We know this because an inscription was painted leaving a space for the name of the purchaser. In this case he forgot to fill it in!

# Egypt and Its Neighbors

Protected by sea and desert, Egypt had developed with little foreign influence. Egyptian culture passed into Africa through Kush in Nubia. Eventually the Kushites formed their own kingdom, bringing Egypt's control over their precious resources, namely gold, to an end. Meanwhile Hyksos settlers from western Asia established their own ruling dynasty, with its capital at Avaris in the Nile Delta.

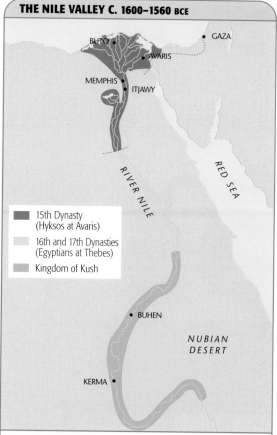

**THE NILE VALLEY C. 1600–1560 BCE**

- 15th Dynasty (Hyksos at Avaris)
- 16th and 17th Dynasties (Egyptians at Thebes)
- Kingdom of Kush

BUTO — GAZA — AVARIS — MEMPHIS — ITJAWY — RIVER NILE — RED SEA — BUHEN — NUBIAN DESERT — KERMA

**The Kingdom of Kush**

The gold of Nubia, and its trade routes to the luxuries of tropical Africa attracted armed Egyptian expeditions. In defence, the Nubians formed the kingdom of Kush, based on the Egyptian state, about 1560 BCE. The kingdom competed with Egypt for control over the Nile.

*Nubians shared the Egyptians' taste for beautiful objects, like this jar in the form of an antelope.*

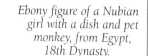

*Ebony figure of a Nubian girl with a dish and pet monkey, from Egypt, 18th Dynasty.*

**Divided Kingship**

*At the end of the Middle Kingdom Egypt lost power and the Nile Valley was divided into several kingdoms. The kingdom of Kush lay to the south, in Nubia, while the Hyksos ruled from Avaris (14th and 15th Dynasties) in the Delta. Central Egypt was ruled by Egyptians, from Thebes (16th and 17th Dynasties).*

*Nubian archers on the march, from a wooden model found in a tomb.*

## Trade with Kush

Nubian gold and slaves, as well as the luxury goods that came from further south passed through Kerma, the first Kushite capital. Kerma was a center for trade over a wide region. The Egyptians levied taxes, or tributes, in gold and slaves, from the Nubian chiefs whom they controlled, or paid for them in grain.

*A wall painting from Thebes showing a Nubian princess bringing gifts to pharaoh.*

*Pyramids at Meroe, an example of the Kushites' adoption of Egyptian customs.*

## The Hyksos

During the Second Intermediate Period (1782–1570 BCE) foreigners from western Asia who had settled in Egypt gained power and ruled part of Egypt. Manetho called these rulers of the 15th Dynasty "Hyksos," but the Egyptians called them "Rulers of the Foreign Lands." The Hyksos established their capital at Avaris (Tell el-Dab'a) and eventually took control of Memphis. They had superior military technology and it is believed that they introduced the use of horse-drawn chariots.

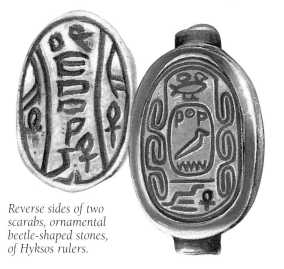

*Reverse sides of two scarabs, ornamental beetle-shaped stones, of Hyksos rulers.*

## Neighbors and Enemies

Pharaohs of the 18th Dynasty, after driving out the foreign Hyksos rulers, conquered nearby lands for greater protection. They had contacts, some friendly some hostile, with Assyrians, Babylonians, Hittites (powerful enemies), Libyans, and Mycenaeans. Queen Hatshepsut traded with the kingdom of Punt in East Africa, which was reached by ships sailing down the Red Sea. From Punt the Egyptians obtained slaves, gold, and incense.

*Detail of a painted stone relief showing men from Punt bringing goods to Egypt.*

## COMPETING DYNASTIES

**C. 1700 BCE**
*During the last years of the 13th Dynasty, rulers of the 14th Dynasty rule at the same time from the eastern Delta. The kingdom of Kush is founded in Nubia.*

**C. 1669 BCE**
*The kingdom of the Hyksos at Avaris is founded (15th Dynasty).*

**1663 BCE**
*The 17th Dynasty is founded at Thebes.*

**1573–1570 BCE**
*Reign of the pharaoh Kamose, who attacks the Hyksos rulers at Avaris.*

**1520 BCE**
*Pharaoh Ahmose I (reigned 1570–1546) of the 18th Dynasty (New Kingdom) defeats the Hyksos Kingdom at Avaris.*

**C. 1500–1000 BCE**
*Kush becomes an Egyptian province.*

**C. 1460 BCE**
*Queen Hatshepsut sends an expedition to Punt.*

**C. 715–663 BCE**
*Kushites rule Egypt as 25th Dynasty.*

**C. 592 BCE**
*New Kushite capital is established at Meroe.*

*A jeweler's workshop. Some men use bow drills to make holes in beads for a necklace.*

### Craftworkers

The Egyptians were a practical people. Extraordinary skills were needed to develop the calendar, build a pyramid, or mummify a body. Craftsmen learned their trade from their fathers. Among the most skillful were furniture makers, potters, jewelers, and glassmakers.

### Food and Farming

Farming was the chief business of the mass of the people—the peasants. They grew wheat and barley, from which they made oven-baked bread and beer, and corn, which they used to pay rent. Besides flax, for linen clothes, they grew vegetables (lettuce, onions, beans, turnips) and fruit (figs, dates, grapes, pomegranates, melons). They kept cattle, for meat and milk, sheep, goats, pigs, geese, ducks, and pigeons (but no chickens).

*The Egyptian plow was simply a heavy spike, which cut long, narrow tracks in the soil.*

# Daily Life in Ancient Egypt

**W**e know more about the everyday lives of the Egyptians than most other ancient people thanks to the records, in pictures and writing, in tombs. Family life was important. We see gestures of affection between man and wife and for children and animals, especially cats, which were identified with the goddess Bastet. The Egyptians enjoyed food and drink, parties, sport, and board games. But the most common subject of daily life is farming.

*A woman's make-up box containing cosmetics, such as kohl for darkening the eyes.*

### Houses

Peasants' houses were built of mud bricks. They were small, dark, and high-walled, with two or three rooms and stairs to the flat roof, where people spent much of their time. Richer people lived in villas with many rooms, decorated with paintings and tiles, with separate servants' quarters and sometimes a flower garden (the world's first).

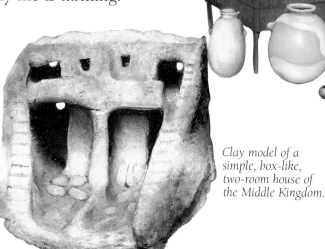

*Clay model of a simple, box-like, two-room house of the Middle Kingdom.*

### Clothes

Thanks to the climate, the Egyptians did not need many clothes. Workmen wore only a loin cloth, children often nothing at all. Clothes were usually made from linen, which could be woven into cloth so fine it was almost transparent. Clothes remained simple and were usually white, though in the Middle Kingdom colored, patterned dresses appeared.

## Children

For the Egyptians, to be neat and clean was a religious duty. Children often had their heads shaved, except for a decorative tress or two. Only a few went to school. Most learned about life, work, and religion at home. They had toys and dolls and played the same sort of games as Egyptian children today.

*Musicians played stringed (such as lute and harp) and wind instruments (wooden pipes, trumpets).*

## Entertainment

Rich people enjoyed parties and feasts. They were waited on by young women, who entertained them with music and dancing. Other entertainers included jugglers, acrobats, and clowns. Women wore wigs with a cone of greasy substance on top that gradually melted, giving off a pleasing scent of myrrh.

*Family life was close. Children and women were respected, although a man was allowed to have more than one wife.*

*This toy horse could be pulled along by a string through its nose.*

**NEW KINGDOM TRADE ROUTES**

- Area of Egyptian control
- Near Eastern trade routes
- Supposed trade routes
- Nubian caravans
- Punt trade routes

**Trade Routes**

*The Nile River carried internal trade, and led to the Mediterranean and foreign trade routes. The desert roads, west and south, were older. During the Middle Kingdom, the Egyptians traveled from Aswan on the Nile to Darfur, bringing back ebony, ivory, and a "dancing dwarf."*

*Traders on the way to market with wild fowl, hunted in the delta, and wine.*

## Means of Exchange

As money did not exist, most trade was barter, or exchange of goods. However, traders could calculate the relative value of goods by known units, such as bags of grain of a standard size, or copper (or gold) of a certain weight. If someone bought a dried fish for a deben of copper, payment was not made in copper, but something of equivalent value.

## Imports and Exports

Thanks to the fertility of the land, the Egyptians produced enough grain to feed themselves and sell to others. Another export was papyrus, an early form of paper made from reeds. Imports included cedarwood, which came from Lebanon. Metals and precious stones came from the desert. One favorite, lapis lazuli, originated in Afghanistan.

# Trading on the Nile

The rich country of Egypt provided most of the products ordinary people needed, but some goods had to be imported from other lands. For example, wood was scarce (few trees grew in Egypt) and was brought from Lebanon. The Egyptians obtained valuable minerals, including gold, from the desert oases and from Nubia in the south (see page 17). In a time when iron was not to be had, all the Egyptians' copper, the metal from which tools and weapons were made, came from Sinai.

*A spoon for cosmetic powder, carved in elephant ivory from East Africa.*

*A treasury official weighs gold rings. Cheating was not easy, and scales like these were very accurate.*

## Quaysides

As everyone lived near the river, which was also the highway for trade, markets grew up on the quaysides. Pictures in tombs show that these markets were visited by foreign merchants, but they were mostly for local trade and were Egypt's only "shopping centers." Besides regular traders, craftsmen, local fishermen, and farmers' wives would come to buy and sell surplus products.

*People of many sorts mingled at the quayside market.*

### TRADE

**c. 3800 BCE**
*Early trade contacts between Egypt and Mesopotamia and Syria.*

**c. 3200 BCE**
*Earliest record of Egyptian sea voyages; copper brought from Sinai.*

**c. 3100 BCE**
*Military expeditions to Nubia to mine gold.*

**c. 2300 BCE**
*Harkhuf (active c. 2290–2270 BCE), governor of Upper Egypt, leads expedition to southern Nubia with 300 donkeys: 100 carried water, the rest brought back incense, ebony, "panthers," ivory, and other goods.*

**c. 1500 BCE**
*Increasing trade with countries throughout the eastern Mediterranean region.*

**c. 1492 BCE**
*First voyage to "Punt" (probably Somalia) via the Nile and the Red Sea, where the ships were built. They brought back myrrh (incense) trees, ivory, ebony, and other rare woods, and live baboons, in exchange for jewelry and weapons.*

**c. 500 BCE**
*An 53-mile 85-km canal was built between the Nile and the Red Sea.*

## Nile Boats

Small boats for short journeys were made of bundles of papyrus reeds. Larger vessels were made of cedarwood, joined by wooden pegs and ropes of tough grass. Seagoing ships had a mast and single sail, plus 12 or more oars each side and steering oars at the stern.

*Sailors carry grain (their wages) off the ship at Thebes. They will exchange some at the market.*

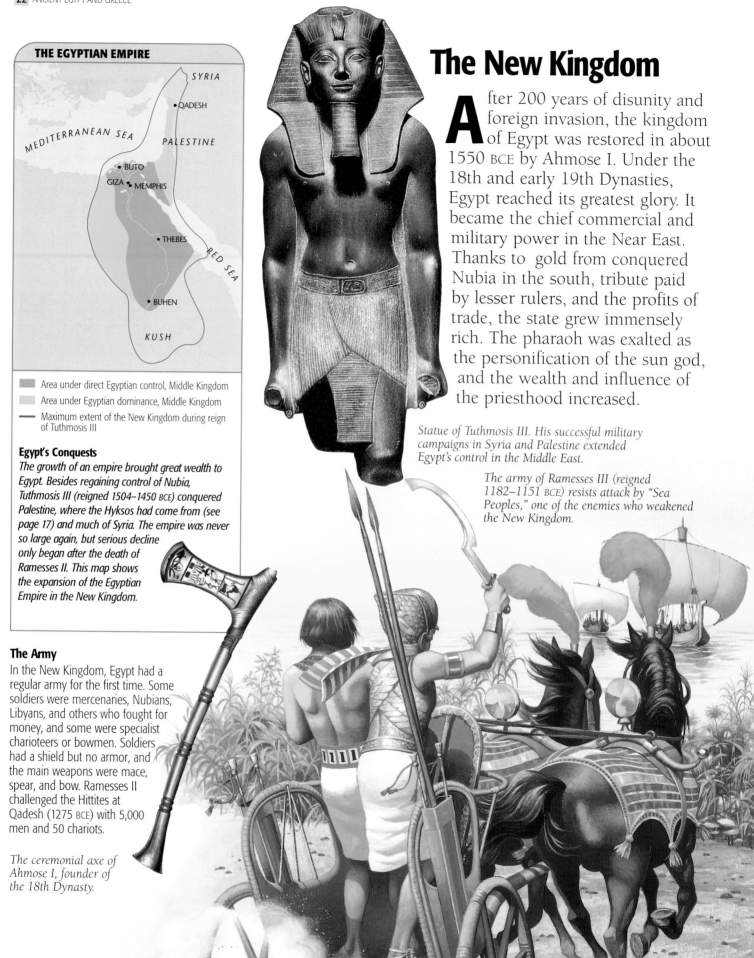

## THE EGYPTIAN EMPIRE

SYRIA

• QADESH

MEDITERRANEAN SEA

PALESTINE

• BUTO

GIZA • MEMPHIS

• THEBES

RED SEA

• BUHEN

KUSH

- ▇ Area under direct Egyptian control, Middle Kingdom
- ▨ Area under Egyptian dominance, Middle Kingdom
- — Maximum extent of the New Kingdom during reign of Tuthmosis III

### Egypt's Conquests

*The growth of an empire brought great wealth to Egypt. Besides regaining control of Nubia, Tuthmosis III (reigned 1504–1450 BCE) conquered Palestine, where the Hyksos had come from (see page 17) and much of Syria. The empire was never so large again, but serious decline only began after the death of Ramesses II. This map shows the expansion of the Egyptian Empire in the New Kingdom.*

### The Army

In the New Kingdom, Egypt had a regular army for the first time. Some soldiers were mercenaries, Nubians, Libyans, and others who fought for money, and some were specialist charioteers or bowmen. Soldiers had a shield but no armor, and the main weapons were mace, spear, and bow. Ramesses II challenged the Hittites at Qadesh (1275 BCE) with 5,000 men and 50 chariots.

*The ceremonial axe of Ahmose I, founder of the 18th Dynasty.*

# The New Kingdom

After 200 years of disunity and foreign invasion, the kingdom of Egypt was restored in about 1550 BCE by Ahmose I. Under the 18th and early 19th Dynasties, Egypt reached its greatest glory. It became the chief commercial and military power in the Near East. Thanks to gold from conquered Nubia in the south, tribute paid by lesser rulers, and the profits of trade, the state grew immensely rich. The pharaoh was exalted as the personification of the sun god, and the wealth and influence of the priesthood increased.

*Statue of Tuthmosis III. His successful military campaigns in Syria and Palestine extended Egypt's control in the Middle East.*

*The army of Ramesses III (reigned 1182–1151 BCE) resists attack by "Sea Peoples," one of the enemies who weakened the New Kingdom.*

## Akhenaten

One of the more famous New Kingdom pharaohs was Amenhotep IV (reigned 1350–1334 BCE). At the beginning of his reign he changed his name to Akhenaten and dedicated a temple near Karnak to Aten, the Sun disk, instead of Amun (the supreme god). He also closed the temple dedicated to Amun. This shocked everyone, in fact, after his death he was labelled a heretic.

*This gold amulet, representing Maat, was found with the mummy of Tutankhamun.*

*Relief showing Akhenaten and Queen Nefertiti with three of their children.*

## Gold

The Egyptians wanted to control Nubia for its luxury trade, above all its gold. Gold came from dry river beds, where it was easily collected, and rocky hills east of the Nile River. It reached Egypt as gold dust or nuggets. Nubian gold paid for the expansion of the empire.

## THE DECLINE

**1570 BCE**
*Beginning of the New Kingdom. Ahmose I consolidates the empire's borders.*

**1483 BCE**
*Death of Queen Hatshepsut. Tuthmosis III, Hatshepsut's co-regent and step-son, assumes full power.*

**1386 BCE**
*Amenhotep III (reigned 1386–1349 BCE) brings prosperity and stability to the empire.*

**1324 BCE**
*Tutankhamun dies and is replaced by Ay (reigned 1324–1319 BCE), the first of the three non-royal army generals to become pharaoh.*

**1279 BCE**
*Ramesses II takes the throne. He orders the building of the great temple at Abu Simbel in Nubia.*

**c. 1177 BCE**
*Invading "Sea Peoples" are driven back by Ramesses III.*

**1069 BCE**
*Beginning of the Third Intermediate Period, with Smendes I (reigned 1069–1043 BCE) of the 21st Dynasty. Tanis, in Lower Egypt, is the new capital.*

**525 BCE**
*Egyptians are defeated by the Persians who take charge of Egypt, founding the 27th Dynasty and marking the beginning of the Late Period.*

**332 BCE**
*Alexander the Great, king of Macedonia (see page 43), invades Egypt.*

## Religion

Minoan religion was closely related to nature. The chief deity was a goddess, whose sign was the double-headed axe of King Minos. The male god, a junior figure, was linked with the bull, a sacred animal. He "died" each fall and was "reborn" in spring. Complicated rituals may have taken place in temples, but most worship was at small household shrines, in the open or in sacred caves.

# The Minoans

The first European civilization arose on the island of Crete over 4,000 years ago and lasted about 600 years. It was a complex society of great palaces and cities, with high living standards based on farming, but gaining its wealth from trade. The people are called Minoans after a legendary king, Minos, who kept a bull-like monster, the Minotaur, in a labyrinth (underground maze). Minoan civilization was entirely unknown until its remains were discovered by archeologists about 100 years ago. As we cannot read the Minoan language, our knowledge comes mainly from their finds.

**THE MINOANS**

**c. 2900–2000 BCE**
*Beginning of early Bronze Age cultures in the Aegean. Inhabitants of the Cyclades, a group of small islands north of Crete, develop their own distinct culture.*

**c. 2100 BCE**
*Rise of Minoan civilization; palaces are built in Crete.*

**c. 1700 BCE**
*Widespread destruction, followed by rebuilding.*

**c. 1600 BCE**
*Rise of Mycenaeans in Greece.*

**c. 1500 BCE**
*Minoan society and art at its peak.*

**c. 1450 BCE**
*Major disaster (earthquake?), followed by Mycenaean takeover.*

*This fine ewer or pitcher, with a pattern based on leaves of grass, comes from the palace of Phaistos.*

*A scene from a Minoan tomb with priestesses taking part in a religious ceremony.*

*Minoan ships were up to 30 m (98 ft) long, with oars and a sail. They also shipped goods for other peoples.*

**THE ANCIENT AEGEAN**

- TROY

ASIA MINOR

- DELPHI
- CORINTH
- MYCENAE

PYLOS - SPARTA

CYCLADES

MEDITERRANEAN SEA

AEGEAN SEA

KNOSSOS

CRETE

■ Cycladic Island Culture c. 2500–1900 BCE
■ Minoan Culture c. 2000–1400 BCE
— Mycenaean Culture c. 1600–1150 BCE

## Crete

*Although Crete was said to contain 100 towns, the island is only about 155 miles 250 km long, east to west, and 34 miles (55 km) across at the widest. It has many good harbors, where sailors took refuge from the earliest times. It is very mountainous, and only about one-quarter was farmed, but the land was so fertile it supported a large population.*

## Trade and the Sea

Minoan Crete was a sea power. Its navy kept the island safe from attack, its trade made it wealthy, and its colonies provided agents and bases abroad. The Minoans' finest manufactures—pottery, jewelry, metal wares—have been found throughout the eastern Mediterranean. They also exported food, olive oil, and cloth. Egypt was their biggest customer. The Minoans imported gold and other metals, along with ivory and fine stone.

## Architecture

The most remarkable buildings of ancient Crete were the Minoan palaces, which were like small towns and the centers of economic life, religion, and government. They had no defensive walls, as the Minoans did not fear attack. City streets were paved, with a piped water supply and sewage system.

*Images of Minoan houses, which were square, flat-roofed, and sometimes with several floors.*

## Knossos

The palace of Knossos was up to five floors high and covered the area of two football fields. The buildings, around a courtyard, housed thousands of people. Living quarters were on the light and airy upper floors. Besides elegant court chambers, beautifully decorated with frescoes (wall paintings), the palace contained shrines, workshops, storerooms, and offices.

*The Queen's Hall at Knossos was decorated with a painting of dolphins.*

THE MYCENAEANS

*The Mycenaeans were strongly influenced by the Minoans. This Mycenaean krater shows an octopus: a Minoan favourite.*

**c. 3000–2000 BCE**
*Ancestors of the Mycenaeans settle in Greece.*

**c. 1600 BCE**
*Mycenaeans begin to trade with Minoans.*

**c. 1500 BCE**
*Mycenaeans begin to use chariots.*

**c. 1400 BCE**
*Mycenaeans control Crete.*

**c. 1250 BCE**
*The city of Troy is captured.*

**c. 1150 BCE**
*Collapse of Mycenaean civilization, cities deserted.*

# The Mycenaeans

Soon after 1450 BCE Crete was taken over by the Mycenaeans, the dominant people of mainland Greece from before 1600 BCE, who are named after their largest city. A stronger, more warlike people than the Minoans, they inherited the Minoan trading empire and enlarged it, with bases throughout the eastern Mediterranean. They lived in independent cities, which sometimes acted together but sometimes fought each other. In each city, the king was supported by landowning warriors, who ruled over craftsmen, peasants, and slaves.

### Fortified Cities

Built on hilltops, Mycenaean cities (unlike Minoan) were strongly fortified, with stone walls up to 20 feet (6 m) thick. At the center was the citadel, containing the royal palace. The city was the center of government and the economy, controlling a large area of farm land.

*The entrance, known as the Lion Gate, to the citadel at Mycenae.*

### Writing

We cannot read the Minoan script, called Linear A. But about 1400 BCE another system, Linear B, appeared in Crete. This was famously deciphered in the 1950s, when the language turned out to be an early form of Greek, which was used by the Mycenaeans.

*Written records were made on clay tablets. Thousands have survived thanks to their being fired, which hardened the clay.*

*A bronze suit of armor that must have belonged to a king or great warrior.*

### Warfare

The Mycenaeans were warriors. Shaft graves contained many weapons, and walls were decorated with battle scenes. They learned chariot warfare from Egypt, and fought with spear and sword. They wore helmets and leather or bronze armor, with huge, body-length shields. The northerners who finally overcame them probably had iron weapons, superior to bronze.

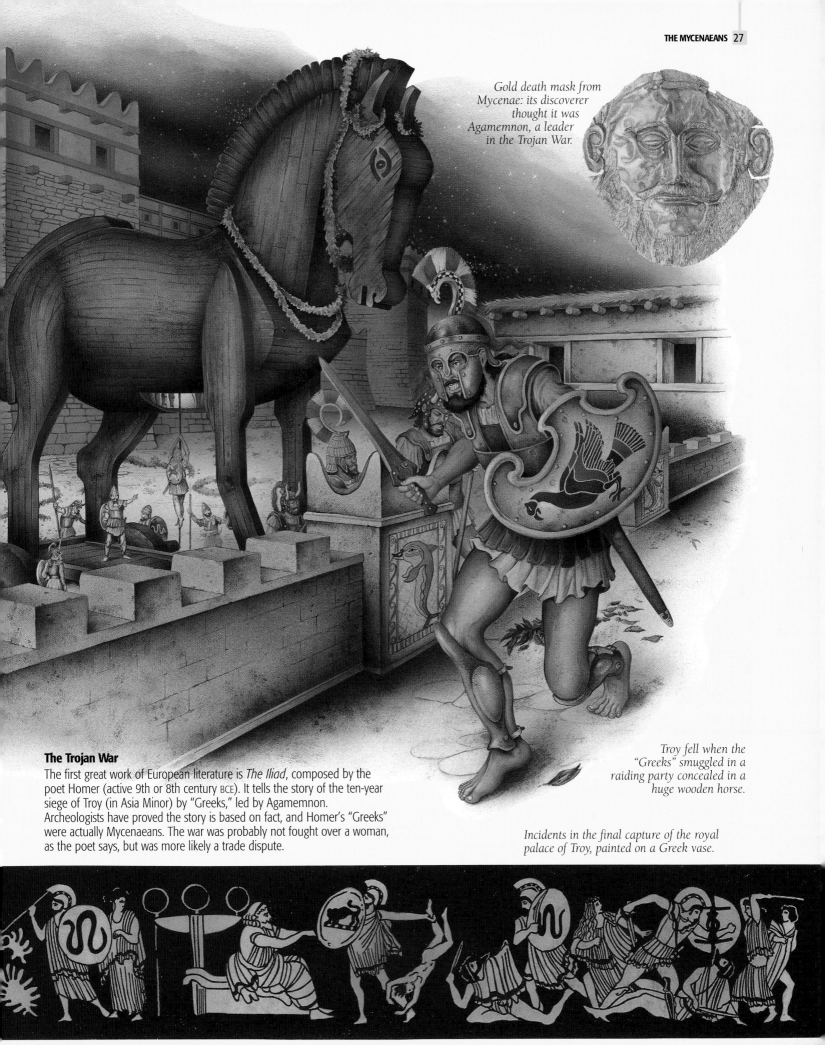

Gold death mask from Mycenae: its discoverer thought it was Agamemnon, a leader in the Trojan War.

## The Trojan War

The first great work of European literature is *The Iliad*, composed by the poet Homer (active 9th or 8th century BCE). It tells the story of the ten-year siege of Troy (in Asia Minor) by "Greeks," led by Agamemnon. Archeologists have proved the story is based on fact, and Homer's "Greeks" were actually Mycenaeans. The war was probably not fought over a woman, as the poet says, but was more likely a trade dispute.

Troy fell when the "Greeks" smuggled in a raiding party concealed in a huge wooden horse.

Incidents in the final capture of the royal palace of Troy, painted on a Greek vase.

## Greece: The Dark Age

**Lefkandi**

At Lefkandi, on the island of Euboea, archeologists recently found evidence of great prosperity during the Dark Age. About 1000 BCE, Lefkandi had overseas trade, a metalworking industry, and a large building that resembled the future Greek temples. Graves contained valuable and beautiful objects, some imported. There may be other such places, still undiscovered.

**M**ycenaean civilization disappeared quickly and almost completely. Within 100 years, trade ceased, cities fell into ruins, population dropped sharply, and people were much poorer. There were no more clay tablets—no written records—for the art of writing was forgotten. Darkness fell on Greece. For over three centuries, so far as we can tell, life seems to have been grim. But there were bright spots. A few Mycenaeans settled successfully in Cyprus and some places, such as Lefkandi, recovered much sooner.

*Clay model of a centaur (half man, half horse), found in a tomb at Lefkandi.*

*Bards played a vital part in spreading and strengthening the Greeks' idea of themselves as a special people.*

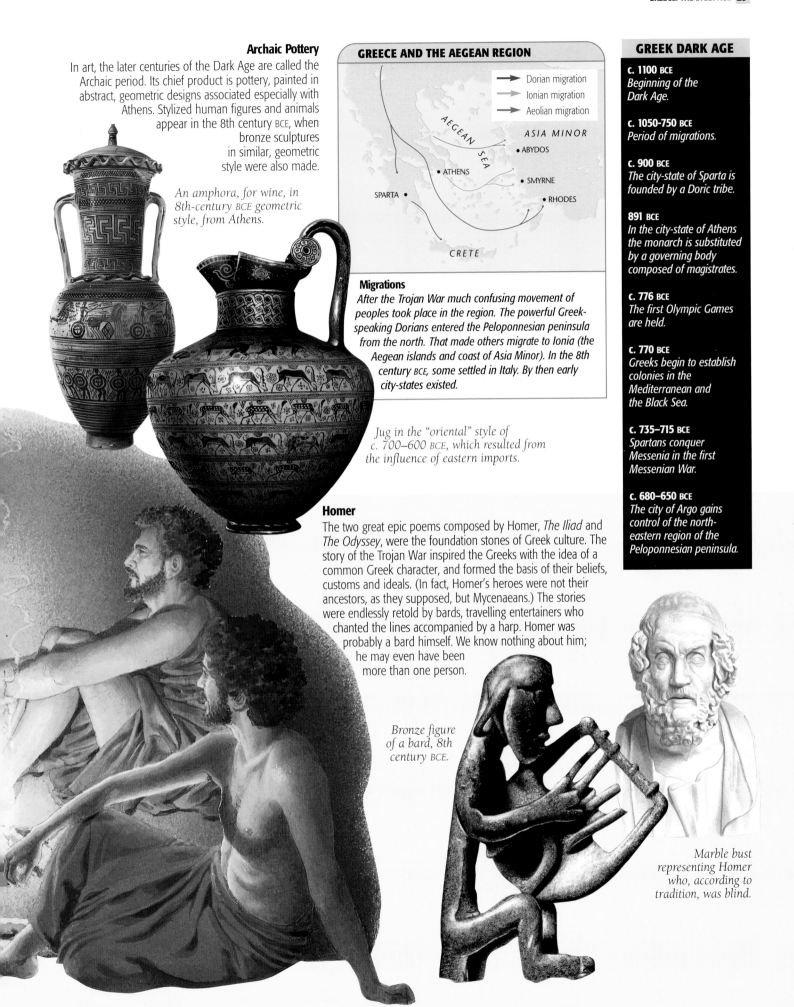

## Archaic Pottery

In art, the later centuries of the Dark Age are called the Archaic period. Its chief product is pottery, painted in abstract, geometric designs associated especially with Athens. Stylized human figures and animals appear in the 8th century BCE, when bronze sculptures in similar, geometric style were also made.

*An amphora, for wine, in 8th-century BCE geometric style, from Athens.*

### GREECE AND THE AEGEAN REGION

→ Dorian migration
→ Ionian migration
→ Aeolian migration

AEGEAN SEA

ASIA MINOR
• ABYDOS
• ATHENS
• SMYRNE
SPARTA •
• RHODES

CRETE

## Migrations

After the Trojan War much confusing movement of peoples took place in the region. The powerful Greek-speaking Dorians entered the Peloponnesian peninsula from the north. That made others migrate to Ionia (the Aegean islands and coast of Asia Minor). In the 8th century BCE, some settled in Italy. By then early city-states existed.

*Jug in the "oriental" style of c. 700–600 BCE, which resulted from the influence of eastern imports.*

## Homer

The two great epic poems composed by Homer, *The Iliad* and *The Odyssey*, were the foundation stones of Greek culture. The story of the Trojan War inspired the Greeks with the idea of a common Greek character, and formed the basis of their beliefs, customs and ideals. (In fact, Homer's heroes were not their ancestors, as they supposed, but Mycenaeans.) The stories were endlessly retold by bards, travelling entertainers who chanted the lines accompanied by a harp. Homer was probably a bard himself. We know nothing about him; he may even have been more than one person.

*Bronze figure of a bard, 8th century BCE.*

*Marble bust representing Homer who, according to tradition, was blind.*

### GREEK DARK AGE

**c. 1100 BCE**
*Beginning of the Dark Age.*

**c. 1050-750 BCE**
*Period of migrations.*

**c. 900 BCE**
*The city-state of Sparta is founded by a Doric tribe.*

**891 BCE**
*In the city-state of Athens the monarch is substituted by a governing body composed of magistrates.*

**c. 776 BCE**
*The first Olympic Games are held.*

**c. 770 BCE**
*Greeks begin to establish colonies in the Mediterranean and the Black Sea.*

**c. 735–715 BCE**
*Spartans conquer Messenia in the first Messenian War.*

**c. 680–650 BCE**
*The city of Argo gains control of the north-eastern region of the Peloponnesian peninsula.*

## THE CLASSICAL AGE

**508 BCE**
*Beginning of democracy in Athens.*

**c. 500 BCE**
*Beginning of the Classical age.*

**478 BCE**
*Formation of the Delian League, dominated by Athens, which profits from tribute-paying members.*

**432 BCE**
*Spartans establish a military alliance with other city-states, called the Peloponnesian League, in order to resist Persian invasions and to ally against Athens.*

**431–404 BCE**
*The Peloponnesian War (Athens vs. Sparta).*

# Classical Greece

During the Classical age in Greece, c. 500–300 BCE, a combination of individuals of huge ability, living in a society that encouraged thought and the arts, lifted human society to new levels. The warring city-states of Athens and Sparta gained control of large areas beyond their city walls. The Spartans became a great military power while the Athenians flourished in the arts and learning. Like every society, the Greeks learned from earlier civilizations, yet they more or less invented democracy.

## The City-State

The Greeks, with the same language, religion, and customs, shared an idea of "Greekness," but lived in independent city-states, and their first loyalty was to their state, or *polis*. The *polis* was more than a state, it was a kind of living body of the citizens, almost a club—but for men only. Women, slaves and foreigners were excluded. Many of these communities were small enough for the citizens to all know each other.

## Athens and Sparta

Although they might combine against a common enemy, the two greatest Greek cities were intense rivals. Athens was the cultural heart of the Greek world; it was democratic, tolerant, and intellectually curious. Sparta, in contrast, belonged to an older tradition, and was authoritarian and militaristic, with a huge underclass of helots, who were really the slaves of the state. Sparta had the most formidable army, Athens the best navy.

*A herdsman tends his goats outside Athens, with the Acropolis, or citadel, in the distance.*

*A Spartan hoplite (soldier). All male Spartan citizens were trained soldiers.*

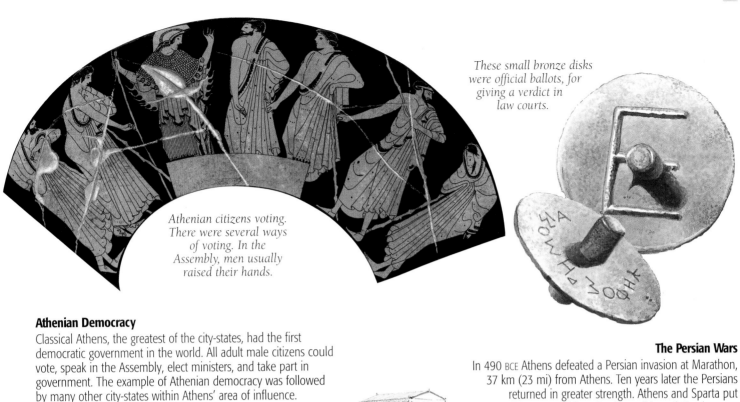

*Athenian citizens voting. There were several ways of voting. In the Assembly, men usually raised their hands.*

*These small bronze disks were official ballots, for giving a verdict in law courts.*

## Athenian Democracy

Classical Athens, the greatest of the city-states, had the first democratic government in the world. All adult male citizens could vote, speak in the Assembly, elect ministers, and take part in government. The example of Athenian democracy was followed by many other city-states within Athens' area of influence. Others looked to Sparta, still ruled by a king and nobles.

## The Persian Wars

In 490 BCE Athens defeated a Persian invasion at Marathon, 37 km (23 mi) from Athens. Ten years later the Persians returned in greater strength. Athens and Sparta put differences aside to lead a coalition of Greek states. They defeated the Persian fleet at Salamis in 480 BCE and the Persian army at Plataea in 479 BCE. Their success stimulated Greek confidence and the rise of Athens.

*The feats of the mighty Greek army were also celebrated in art. This late classical wine jar from Athens shows a Greek soldier (right) taking on three Persian soldiers.*

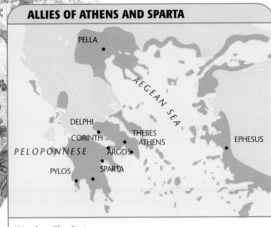

### ALLIES OF ATHENS AND SPARTA

PELLA

AEGEAN SEA

DELPHI

CORINTH THEBES
ATHENS

PELOPONNESE ARGOS

PYLOS SPARTA

EPHESUS

## Warring City-States

*After the Persian Wars Athens became the leader of a confederation of states, with headquarters on the island of Delos, known as the Delian League. Members of the league followed the same military strategy and all contributed to a common fund. Athens soon took control of the funds and dominated the member states, creating an Athenian Empire. In response, Sparta formed allies of her own. Conflict soon erupted and the Peloponnesian War began (see page 42).*

▇ Sparta and allies
▇ Athenian Empire
▇ Athenian allies

*Rougher sports included cock-fighting; here, men try to make a cat fight a dog.*

## Sport

The Greeks believed in healthy minds and bodies. Children played vigorous ball games. Men went to gymnasiums and played team games (a painting of one looks like hockey). Regular athletic meetings took place all over Greece. They probably had a religious meaning at first, as the Olympic Games took place at Olympia, the home of the gods.

*Visitors from other parts changed their currency at a stall in the agora. This is an Athenian coin.*

## The Agora

Every city contained an open space, the agora, near the center. Most male citizens would visit it at some time of day to discuss business or hear the gossip. It was often lined by shady colonnades, with offices, law courts, and shops behind them, and it was here that public monuments and memorials were put up.

# Daily Life in Ancient Greece

Although men respected women, they were in charge. A woman could not own property or carry out business. She lived under the control of her husband, who was chosen by her father, or, if single, of a male relative. Men and women had separate living quarters. Upper-class wives were expected to stay at home to run the household, grind corn, and weave cloth. Husbands or servants did the shopping. Men were away all day, working or socialising. In spite of this inequality, paintings and literature show that family life was often close and affectionate.

## Clothing

People wore simple, loose clothes, made at home. A woman's chiton was a rectangle of cloth passed around the body and fixed with shoulder pins. Men wore a similar loose tunic, sometimes knee-length. Nudity was not offensive: children and young men sometimes wore nothing. Footwear, if any, was sandals or soft boots. Men wore a broad-brimmed hat when traveling.

*Clothes and other things were stored in chests, not cupboards.*

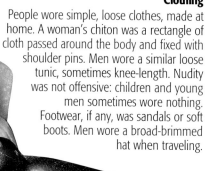
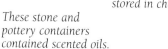

*These stone and pottery containers contained scented oils.*

*In the women's quarters: weaving, hairstyling, and playing games with the children.*

*A mother with her child, who is sitting in a potty chair (the pot is in the base).*

## Children

Many children died at birth or as babies, but parents were eager to have them, especially boys, who were considered more valuable. Children lived in the women's quarters until aged about seven, when sons (but not daughters) of citizens went to school. Other boys, and most girls, learned from their parents. Childhood ended at about age 15.

*A spoon with animal-head handle, perhaps for a child.*

## Homes

Houses were built of mud bricks, around a central courtyard. Furniture was scanty—couches (used when eating as well as sleeping), stools (seldom chairs), and three-legged tables. Objects such as tools or musical instruments were hung on walls, which often had a painted decorative band running around the room.

# Trade and Colonies

In Greece, as in other ancient societies, the most important business was farming, and farming employed the largest number of people. But the mountainous countryside and hot, dry climate made good farming land scarce. Few crops except olives and grapes grew well. The Greeks therefore had to import much of their food, especially grain, from other countries. From the 8th century BCE onward, the shortage of good land, and the growing population, drove many Greeks to settle abroad. These colonies became useful centers of trade.

## Trade

Overland travel was slow, difficult, and dangerous, and all trade went by sea. The largest import was grain. Athens imported two-thirds of the grain it needed. In exchange it traded manufactures such as painted pottery and olive oil. Traders were usually independent merchants with their own ship. One typical trader's cargo included scent bottles from Corinth, hides from Euboea, salt fish from the Black Sea, and wine from Chios.

*The Greek cities issued their own coins, which were based on weight (the drachma). The variety of coins made exchange complicated.*

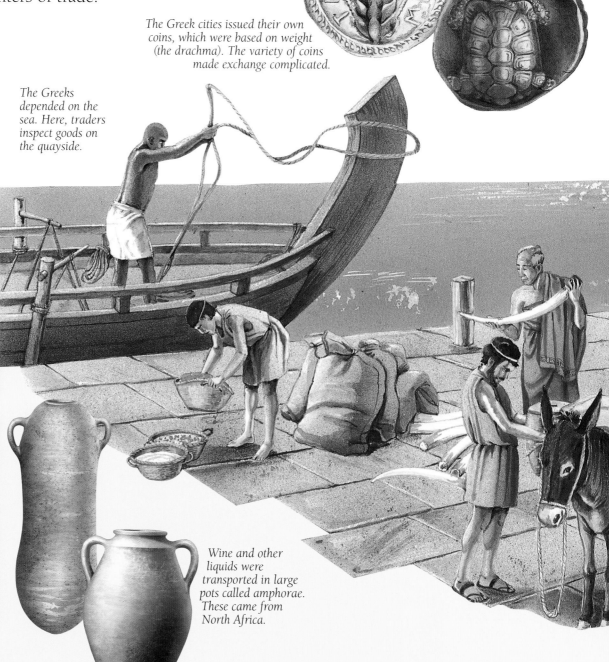

*The Greeks depended on the sea. Here, traders inspect goods on the quayside.*

*Wine and other liquids were transported in large pots called amphorae. These came from North Africa.*

## GREEKS AT SEA

**c. 1050 BCE**
First Greek migrations to Asia Minor.

**c. 750 BCE**
The Italian colony of Tarentum (Taranto) is founded by Spartan settlers.

**c. 730 BCE**
The colony of Syracuse is founded by Corinthians in Sicily.

**c. 630 BCE**
Ionians from Thera settle at Cyrene.

**c. 600 BCE**
Ionians settle at Massalia (modern Marseilles). Development of sail-powered, specialist merchant ships.

**c. 500 BCE**
Ionian revolt against Persian rule.

**c. 483 BCE**
The great politician and naval strategist Themistocles (c. 524–c. 460 BCE) makes Athens a sea power.

**c. 450 BCE**
Piraeus, Athens' port, becomes the chief trading port. Athenian navy crushes pirates.

## Farming

Although some wheat was grown, the main cereal was barley. Farmers raised peas, beans, onions, and cabbages in small plots. They kept goats mainly for milk, sheep mainly for wool, and mules and donkeys for work. Meat, a luxury, came from goats and pigs. Having no sugar, the Greeks kept bees for honey.

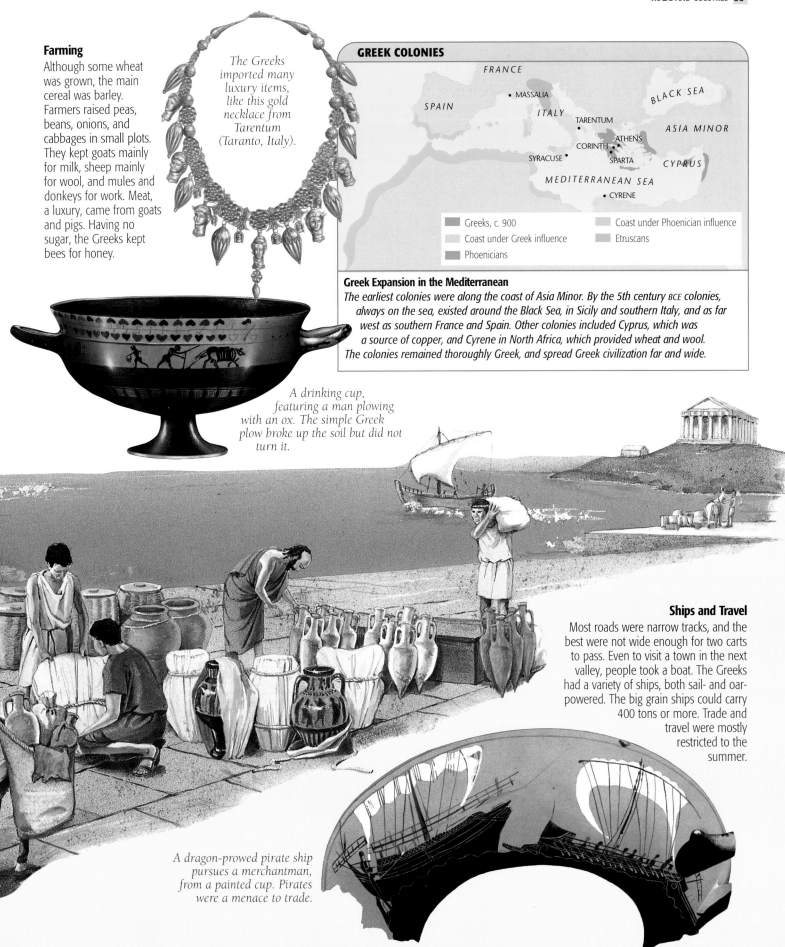

*The Greeks imported many luxury items, like this gold necklace from Tarentum (Taranto, Italy).*

## GREEK COLONIES

### Greek Expansion in the Mediterranean

*The earliest colonies were along the coast of Asia Minor. By the 5th century BCE colonies, always on the sea, existed around the Black Sea, in Sicily and southern Italy, and as far west as southern France and Spain. Other colonies included Cyprus, which was a source of copper, and Cyrene in North Africa, which provided wheat and wool. The colonies remained thoroughly Greek, and spread Greek civilization far and wide.*

Greeks, c. 900
Coast under Greek influence
Phoenicians
Coast under Phoenician influence
Etruscans

*A drinking cup, featuring a man plowing with an ox. The simple Greek plow broke up the soil but did not turn it.*

## Ships and Travel

Most roads were narrow tracks, and the best were not wide enough for two carts to pass. Even to visit a town in the next valley, people took a boat. The Greeks had a variety of ships, both sail- and oar-powered. The big grain ships could carry 400 tons or more. Trade and travel were mostly restricted to the summer.

*A dragon-prowed pirate ship pursues a merchantman, from a painted cup. Pirates were a menace to trade.*

# Learning and Theater

In intellectual and artistic achievement, the Greeks, a uniquely creative people, were pioneers. Although they owed some ideas to other peoples, such as the Egyptians and the Phoenicians (who devised the alphabet), they practically invented epic poetry, drama, history, and philosophy, and they achieved a degree of excellence in those and other fields which no later age has surpassed. In spite of their limited information about the world and nature, they made such progress in science (or natural history) and medicine that no further great advance was made for about 1,500 years.

*Statue of Chrysippus (c. 280– c. 206 BCE), a leader of the school of philosophers known as the Stoics.*

## Science

Greek thinkers were always seeking the causes of things. Their lively minds created wonderful theories, usually logical though often wrong, like the beautiful idea of the Universe as a series of spheres. Aristotle, who taught that collecting facts must come before forming theories, founded biology. Mathematicians included Pythagoras (active 6th century BCE) and Euclid (active c. 300 BCE). Hippocrates (c. 460–c. 377 BCE) was the father of medicine.

## Literature

The love of knowledge and the freedom to seek it produced several "schools" of philosophy and some of the greatest thinkers who ever lived. Among them were Socrates (c. 470–399 BCE); his pupil Plato (c. 428–c. 348 BCE), who wrote *The Republic*, the first account of a state organized on sound principles; and the great Aristotle (384–322 BCE). The Greeks also produced fiction, such as *Aesop's Fables*, and the first true history.

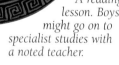

*A reading lesson. Boys might go on to specialist studies with a noted teacher.*

*The abacus, the first calculator, was used by the Egyptians before the Greeks.*

*A doctor with his assistant and patient. This carving was a "thank-you" to Asclepius, god of medicine.*

## Education

Sons of citizens (adult males) went to school where they learned to read and write and also studied arithmetic, poetry, music, and gymnastics. School lasted from age 7 to about 15. It was not free, but fees were low. Probably, many girls learned to read at home. Education varied. In Sparta it was hard, even brutal, as the purpose was to breed toughness.

## Theater

Greek drama grew from religious ritual. The greatest dramas were the tragedies of Aeschylus (c. 525–c. 456 BCE), Sophocles (c. 496–406 BCE), and Euripides (c. 484–406 BCE). The Greeks liked comedies too, and audiences in the open-air theaters watched several plays in a day. They sat on benches cut into a hill in a semicircle around the stage. Actors (men only) wore masks; little action happened on stage; a chorus provided a commentary; there was no scenery, but music was important.

*Dancing and music filled interludes at the theater, as in this Archaic carving.*

*An acrobat in a comedy, on a 4th-century BCE Athenian red-figure vase.*

*It was a citizen's duty to attend the theater, and a man could reclaim any lost wages.*

*Fifth-century BCE bronze statue of a warrior found off the coast of Italy.*

*A carved head in the stiffer, less natural style of the Archaic period.*

# Art and Architecture

In art, the Greeks pursued an ideal, a perfection based on unchanging mathematical standards that govern shape and proportion. The artists' chief subject was mankind—the human form—which was also the form of the gods. Classical art strove for utter realism, reaching a peak in sculptures of the human (chiefly male) nude, and it set the standard for Western art for over 2,000 years. Few sculptures have survived, but we know others from later copies. Less durable art, such as paintings, has long vanished.

## Sculpture

The favorite material of sculptors was bronze, but in later times bronze sculptures were melted down for the metal. We know the names of some sculptors but have nothing of their work. The works we do have were mostly buried or lost at sea, and recovered in recent times. Stone sculpture from buildings has survived better, especially in the decorative friezes running around temples, such as the Parthenon.

*Figures from the Parthenon. The folds of cloth indicate the sculptor's skill and keen observation.*

*The Parthenon in Athens is made of marble, but most temples were built of limestone (which is easier to work).*

## Architecture

The features of Classical Greek architecture were boldness and simplicity. Although limited in technique and materials (no mortar, for example), the Greeks had plenty of building stone for their great temples. The design was one of straight lines, developed from wooden buildings and based on the column. The colonnaded buildings were built in the three Classical Orders, fundamental to most Western architecture.

## THE CLASSICAL ORDERS

*The three orders of architecture are named after the people said to have invented them, Doric (Dorians), Ionic (Ionians) and Corinthian (Corinthians). They are defined by the design of the capitals that top the columns. Doric, with plain capitals, is the earliest and purest. Ionic, with scrolled capitals, is more slender and elegant. Corinthian, with a design of leaves, is the last and most elaborate. Athens had both Doric and Ionian orders. The Parthenon is Doric, but the slimness of the columns shows Ionic influence.*

Doric capital

Ionic capital

Corinthian capital

## Vase Painting

Practically no painting has survived, with one important exception: painted pottery. Pottery was illustrated with scenes from mythology and everyday life—providing valuable information. There were two main types: black-figure pottery, with figures painted black against the lighter background of the clay (7th to 6th centuries BCE), and red-figure, with the background painted black and figures in the natural, reddish color of the clay.

*A 7th-century black-figure vase depicting two legendary figures, Achilles and Ajax, playing a board game.*

## Minor Arts

A painter called Zeuxis (active second half of the 5th century BCE) painted grapes so realistic that birds pecked at them, but paintings, on walls or wood panels, have not survived. By 400 BCE the Greeks had developed the art of mosaics, for floors. They were also expert metal-workers, using most of the techniques of later goldsmiths. They made ornamental bronzes and carved gems, stones, and cameos. Even their coins seem to us works of art.

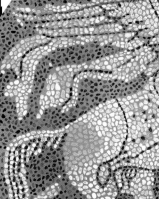

*Mosaics were made of tiny colored pebbles or cubes of stone.*

*Model of the gold and ivory statue of Athena in the Parthenon, which was 40 feet (12 m) high.*

# Religion in Ancient Greece

The Greeks loved order and unity, yet their religion seems very disorderly, with a bewildering number of gods and goddesses. They believed in honor and morality, yet the gods were often silly, cruel, or unjust. However, many of such stories were written later, when gods and religion were less important. In earlier times, religion was everywhere, in every place and event. As we have seen, the great festivals of drama and athletics began as religious ceremonies.

## Gods and Goddesses

The gods of the ancient Greeks had superhuman powers, but they behaved like humans. They had the same pleasures, the same vices, and the same family quarrels in their home on Mount Olympus. They were often associated with a particular state. Athena, for instance, was the patron goddess of Athens, but she was also worshiped, under a different guise, in rival Sparta.

*Detail of a painted vase showing a scene from Homer's* The Odyssey.

## Myths

The Greeks told many stories about gods and superhuman heroes (such as Perseus or Herakles). These stories, which have never lost their fascination, began with Homer (in *The Iliad*, gods and goddesses support both sides in the Trojan War). They are the subject-matter of much Greek art, including sculpture, painted pottery, and the plays of the great 5th-century BCE tragedians.

*A religious procession with a lamb to be sacrificed on an altar near the temple.*

## Festivals

Religious festivals were held to honor the gods. They were times of celebration and included processions, sacrifices, and competitions (athletics, music, drama, etc.). In Athens, festivals occupied 60 days a year. The great summer festival was the Panathenaea (All-Athens Festival), when a new robe woven by the women of Athens was paraded through the city streets to the statue of Athena which stood in the Parthenon.

## Worship and Sacrifice

Worship took place at open-air shrines. Temples were the homes of the gods, and people also provided them with food. They often sacrificed animals—white animals for the Olympians, darker ones for Underworld gods—but ate the best meat themselves. Many priests were part-time, and other leading citizens could act as priests.

*A sacrificial cow: cattle, sheep, goats and pigs were the usual animals for sacrifice.*

## Oracles and Omens

The ancient Greeks believed that it was possible to predict the future, or learn the will of the gods, from omens, like a dream, an eclipse, or any unusual happening. Another way was to examine the liver of a slaughtered animal. These omens were interpreted by professionals. Or you could, for a fee, consult an oracle, notably Apollo's Oracle at Delphi, whose answer was delivered by his priestesses.

*Part of a procession at the Panathenaea, from a sculpture on the Parthenon.*

*The meaning of the Oracle's answer was often unclear. If it proved wrong, you had misunderstood!*

# War and Conquest

The Classical age in Greece began and ended with wars—the Persian Wars and the Peloponnesian War. The Greeks were fine soldiers but not great tacticians. They depended on the formidable phalanx, a tight block of heavy infantry. Alexander the Great introduced new tactics in Asia—lighter, faster infantry, powerful cavalry, and artillery. At sea, warships had a ram to smash the enemy's oars and carried soldiers, who fought hand to hand much like a battle on land.

## Weapons and Armor

Hoplites carried a shield and wore bronze armor—a helmet covering head and face, a cuirass protecting the body and greaves on the lower legs. The phalanx, which aimed to win by sheer force, by breaking the enemy's formation, fought with spears and short swords. Archers and sometimes chariots gave support, but the Greek landscape did not suit cavalry.

*A bronze cuirass or breastplate, made roughly to measure for someone well off.*

*Relief representing the terrifying Medusa from the Greek colony of Syracuse in Sicily. Anyone who looked at her was turned into stone.*

## Armies and Soldiers

Greek hoplites, who fought in the phalanx, were mostly farmers, not professional soldiers, although the Spartans especially were highly trained. Men bought their own armor, handing it down to their sons. By the time of the Peloponnesian War, some states, including Athens, also employed mercenaries (hired soldiers), especially lighter-armed foot soldiers from Thrace, in the north.

*Bronze figure of a mounted soldier, 6th century BCE. He would probably have fought on foot.*

## The Peloponnesian War

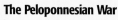

The great civil war for Greek dominance lasted, with intervals, from 431 to 404 BCE. Sparta, aided by its Peloponnesian and Persian allies, feared Athens and its empire in central and eastern Greece. The decisive event was the Athenians' unwise invasion of Sicily in 415 BCE, which led to the loss of most of their young men and eventual surrender. Athens never recovered, and Sparta became the leading state.

### The King of Macedonia

The 18th king of Macedonia, Philip II (382–336 BCE), turned Macedonia into a dominating power thanks to the development of new weapons and clever military tactics and training. The Macedonian army became the world's most powerful military force. Philip II came to the throne in 359 BCE and by 339 BCE he had conquered all of Greece. He was assassinated before he could carry out his plans to invade the Persian Empire in Asia.

*Detail of an ivory statue of King Philip II of Macedonia.*

### Alexander the Great

Philip II was succeeded by his son, Alexander III (356–323 BCE), known as Alexander the Great. As a young man Alexander was taught by the great philosopher Aristotle (see page 36) and by the time he became king, in 336 BCE, he had developed into a unique military genius. His victory over Darius III of Persia (reigned 336–330 BCE) at the Battle of Issus in 333 BCE marked the beginning of his conquest of the Persian Empire.

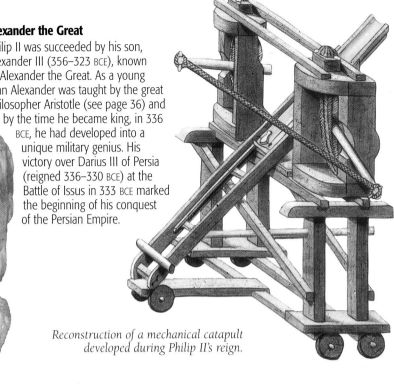

*Reconstruction of a mechanical catapult developed during Philip II's reign.*

*Alexander the Great (far left) portrayed battling King Darius III (centre) in a mosaic copy of a painting of the 4th century BCE.*

**Alexandria**

Among Alexander's many new cities was Alexandria in Egypt, which became the greatest city of the ancient world and the chief center of Hellenistic learning. After Alexander's death, a large library was established in Alexandria. Scholars were invited to live and study there.

*The great lighthouse of Alexandria, one of the Seven Wonders of the ancient world.*

# The Hellenistic Age

Taking up his father's plans, Alexander the Great attacked the vast Persian Empire in 334 BCE and conquered it, from Egypt to Afghanistan, in just five years. Dreaming of a single, peaceful world empire, he pressed on eastward to the Indus River. Though his empire later broke up, Alexander's conquests spread the influence of Greek civilization over a huge area. The time that followed is known as the Hellenistic age (from the Greek word *hellenizein*, meaning "to act like a Greek"), because it was based on Greek culture but included many non-Greeks.

*Alexander the Great and his Hellenes (Greeks). After eight years abroad, his men insisted on going home. Alexander died on the way in 323 BCE, aged 33.*

## Hellenistic Art

The age of Greek culture following the Classical age, from the time of Alexander the Great's death to around the time of the first Roman emperor in 27 BCE, is known as the Hellenistic age. During this time Greek culture spread from the eastern Mediterranean to the Middle East. Hellenistic art flourished in Pella, Rhodes and Athens as well as in Alexandria, Pergamum, and Syracuse.

### THE HELLENISTIC WORLD 240 BCE

- Seleucid Kingdom
- Ptolemaic Kingdom
- Greek city-states
- Antigonid Kingdom

DEAD SEA · CASPIAN SEA · MACEDONIA · BLACK SEA · PELLA · SAMOTHRACE · PERGAMUM · ASIA MINOR · ATHENS · SPARTA · ANTIOCH · MEDITERRANEAN SEA · RHODES · SELEUCIA · BABYLON · ALEXANDRIA · ARABIA · MEMPHIS · EGYPT

### Divided Kingdoms

*After the death of Alexander the Great, his Macedonian generals vied with each other for power. As a result Alexander's empire was divided into three main kingdoms. The Antigonid Kingdom, founded by the general Antigonus I (382–301 BCE), ruled Macedonia and re-established its supremacy over the Greek city-states. The vast Seleucid Empire, which was founded in 312 BCE by Seleucus (c. 358–281 BCE), one of Alexander's most able generals, stretched from Asia Minor to the Indus River. The Ptolemaic Kingdom in Egypt, with its capital at Alexandria, was founded by Ptolemy I (c. 367–c. 283 BCE), another of Alexander's generals. The Ptolemaic Dynasty's reign lasted the longest, falling to the Romans in 30 BCE.*

### The Roman Conquest

The city-state of Rome was established on the Italian peninsula in the mid 8th century BCE. Thanks to its strong army, the Romans had gained control of much of the Mediterranean by the 3rd century BCE. In 168 BCE the Romans won a decisive victory at the Battle of Pydna in which Macedonian forces were crushed. The Romans went on the conquer Greece and the rest of the Hellenistic world.

*A cameo carved inside a cup. Hellenistic art was freer and more expressive, than Classical art.*

*This Hellenistic sculpture of Nike, the winged goddess of victory, comes from Samothrace.*

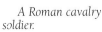
*A Roman cavalry soldier.*

# Glossary

**Amulet** An object or charm that is worn by a person because it is believed to keep away bad luck or evil.

**Archeologist** A scientist who studies the remains of ancient peoples, such as tools, weapons, pots, and buildings, to learn more about cultures of the distant past.

**Archaic** Term used to describe something from the early period of Greek civilization. Something very old.

**Authoritarian** Term used to describe someone or something that makes people follow the rules or laws in a very strict way. A person who gives orders and expects all people to obey him or her.

**Bronze Age** The period in human development following the Stone Age in which people used bronze (instead of just stone) to make weapons and tools.

**Cargo** Goods, transported on a ship or other vehicle, which are traded or sold for profit.

**Chancellor** An official of high rank who, in ancient Egypt, was the head of the government in the earliest times.

**Colony** An area or region controlled and settled by a group of people from a distant country. The ancient Greeks founded colonies to make trading with other states easier and also to acquire raw materials, such as metals, and food supply. Some Greek colonies were independent city-states.

**Confederation** A group of states united for political reasons.

**Crop** A plant or its product, such as grain, fruit or vegetables, grown by farmers.

**Crook** A long stick with a curved end.

**Delta** A triangle-shaped area of land near a river where the waters flow into the sea.

**Democracy** A form of government where ruling representatives are elected by the people.

**Dynasty** A line of rulers coming from the same family, or a period during which they reign.

**Epic** A long poem which tells the story of gods and heroes or the history of a nation or people.

**Faience** Glossy, hard blue or green substance made by heating a mixture of quartz sand with salts and copper powder.

**Flail** A wooden tool made out of a stick that swings from the end of a long handle used in the past to beat grain, separating the seeds from the chaff (unwanted parts).

**Geometric** Term used to describe something decorated with or having the form of simple shapes such as squares, triangles, and circles.

**Headquarters** The place or office where people in charge of a group or organisation work. A command centre.

**Hereditary** Something that is passed on from parent to child.

**Infantry** A group of soldiers who fight on foot with their own personal weapons.

**Labyrinth** A structure of many confusing passages made in such a way so that it is difficult for a person to find his or her way out. A maze.

**Mace** A short heavy stick used as a weapon in ancient times.

**Mercenary** A paid professional soldier who fights for a foreign country.

**Monsoon** A strong wind that brings heavy rains.

**Mourner** A person who expresses deep sorrow or sadness after the death of a person.

**Omen** A message or an event believed to be a sign of a future event.

**Oracle** A sacred place where questions about the future are answered. A person, such as a priest or a priestess, who speaks for a god, answering questions about future events, usually in riddles.

**Phalanx** A group of foot soldiers who march very close together so that their long spears overlap and their shields join to form a protective barrier.

**Procession** The act of a group of people marching in a formal way for a religious ceremony, a ritual parade.

**Propaganda** Specific actions that are carried out or true or false information that is spread to make people have a good opinion about a government or a ruler.

**Province** One of many divisions of a state made by a government to have better control over the territory. In the ancient Roman Empire, conquered lands were made into provinces and were ruled by Roman officials and important local people.

**Pyramid** A large, four-sided triangular stone building constructed in ancient times. In ancient Egypt, the pyramids were built as tombs for the pharaohs, queens, or important people.

**Quarry** A place, usually a pit in the Earth, where minerals and stone are obtained. To obtain building material by digging, cutting, or blasting.

**Quayside** Area of a seaport where boats can dock and load or unload goods.

**Sceptre** A short stick or cane carried by a king or ruler on ceremonial occasions as a symbol of his or her power and authority.

**Scribe** In ancient times, a person who wrote down or recorded important events. A person who copied important documents or manuscripts.

**Sphinx** A mythological creature, sometimes winged, with the body of a lion and the head of a human.

**Tactician** A clever person, usually a military officer, who knows how to lead army or naval forces to get desired results.

**Vizier** A chief minister of ancient Egypt or a high government officer in a Muslim country.

# Index